Lord Maitreya
The Path of Initiation

THE TEMPLE OF THE PRESENCE®

The Ascended Master Wisdom delivered by
Monroe Julius Shearer & Carolyn Louise Shearer

Lord Maitreya:
The Path of Initiation

Published by
Acropolis Sophia Books & Works®
an imprint of
The Temple of The Presence®
P.O. Box 17839, Tucson, Arizona 85731

www.TempleofThePresence.org

Copyright © 2004, 2005, 2021 The Temple of The Presence, Inc.
All rights reserved.
No part of this book may be reproduced
in any form or by any means whatsoever without prior
written permission, except in the case of brief quotations
embodied in articles and reviews.

Cover Art Copyright © 2021 by The Temple of The Presence, Inc.

For information, write
Acropolis Sophia Books & Works®
P.O. Box 17839, Tucson, Arizona 85731

Printed in the United States of America
First Printing, 2021

Library of Congress Control Number: 2020952790
ISBN: 978-1-7337302-6-6

Dictations presented in *The Golden Gifts Series*
have been prepared by the presiding Master for
release in written form for our present use and
for posterity.

Table of Contents

Letter from the Anointed Representatives®.............. *2*

My Instruction on the Path of Initiation................. *5*

When the Student is Ready, the
     Teacher Will Appear................................. *21*

Remarks... *48*

To the Disciple Who Walks the Steep Path to Christhood:

We welcome you to the Crucible of the Heart and to the Ruby Fire of Beloved Lord Maitreya. In the Heart of Maitreya is the intense Love of God as the Ruby Fire and the Wisdom of the Christ. He is known by many as the Cosmic Christ and Planetary Buddha. He is likewise the Great Initiator, and you will find in him one of the greatest Teachers of the mankind of Earth, as well as one of the greatest advocates of the Victory of your Ascension in the Light.

When Lord Maitreya elects to engage more closely with your lifestream, it is a glorious opportunity to accelerate on your Path. Signaled by the nod of your own Mighty I AM Presence, Maitreya will take you by the hand and guide you on the Path of Perfect Love. With his gaze upon you comes the opportunity to step up the vibration of your world, to come into closer communion with your own God Presence, and to strive to accelerate in the Light, bringing more of God into your life.

Sometimes his close proximity can, at first, be most challenging to the student because it often exposes those areas of life that need to be addressed by the Light, karmic momentums that your Presence desires you to be rid of, so they no longer plague your world. But if you stay the course and pass Victorious through the eye of the needle of an Initiation, a wonderful liberation and Freedom will be yours. For you will have come up higher in consciousness and rid yourself of stumbling blocks and boulders in your pathway.

For the student who walks the Steep Path to Christhood that leads to the Ascension in the Light, Lord Maitreya's assistance is most valuable. He holds you in the firm embrace of his Heart. And if you have a fervent love for God, first and foremost, you can be Victorious each and every step of the way.

The Dictations in this book are a roadmap for you as you walk the Path to Christhood. May you always remember that in the Crucible of the Heart you will find your Strength, your Comfort, and your Victory. And with the Love of the Mighty I AM Presence all things are possible.

Know that as you walk this Path in Joy, seeking acceleration and embracing the Fire of the Heart, you will find a Teacher, an advocate, and a most loving Ascended Master Sponsor in Beloved Lord Maitreya.

God Victory unto you!

Monroe Julius Shearer & *Carolyn Louise Shearer*

ANOINTED REPRESENTATIVES®
The Temple of The Presence®

My Instruction on the Path of Initiation
Enter Your Heart

Dear Initiate,

You have elected to enter into the Crucible of Being. You have determined to make this resounding, teaming, Fiery Heart the center of your universe. Indeed it must be, for this is the point upon which you must focus the fullness of your attention in order to enter in through this doorway to the Higher Worlds to discover all that is there waiting for you — and not merely for discovery's sake itself, but for that which you are able to bring into your outer awareness that will become the motor of expression by which you will pass all of the Initiations presented to you, not only by your own Holy Christ Presence, but ultimately by my Heart Flame, should you be elevated to that Cosmic Opportunity for Initiation from the Cosmic Christ.

Become the Initiate of Your Own Holy Christ Presence

For this to come forth, for you to be an initiate of Maitreya, you must first follow suit as an initiate to your own Holy Christ Presence, for these outer vehicles must be trained, tutored, instructed in the Higher Way of Life. This comes first by the Hand of the Holy Christ Presence, by the Mind of the Christ. The heart that beats through the outer vehicle of expression you wear has a Secret Chamber within which resides the Threefold Flame that must be released — for until it is released, the Initiations cannot begin. Your experiences up to that point could be merely the trial and error of the world's buffeting of your own karmic conditions. But, for most of you, this has not been the case for a very long time. For you heard that Inner Call and the Christ has already been released from bondage. The Vibration of the Christ was able to reach through to the outer mind, coursing through your emotional body to reverberate sufficiently to draw you into the proximity of my Instruction.

For most, the Holy Christ Presence is presently attentive to the needs of the hour as determined by that which you are releasing through your being: emotionally charged substance, thoughts that continually pound away, or your calls and pleas expressing your desire for the correction required for you to be able to withstand the karmic circumstances of life.

I AM here to assist you in approaching this Path of Initiation from another perspective so that you might consider what would be for you, as an initiate, an easier path — not easy, but easier to follow and learn, to absorb the Teaching and Instruction, setting aside all sense of struggle and allowing for the Heart, this Crucible of Being, to in fact be at the helm of your endeavors.

Cultivate a Willingness to Learn

For Initiation to come, there must be a willingness to learn. Absent that willingness, there is no room for Initiation, for the consciousness is not receptive to that which would otherwise come forth, either in the passing or the failing of that Initiation. Ofttimes, the greatest learning of an Initiation comes as you progress through the process of that Initiation. It is not learned in the abstract. Oh, how We, the Ascended and Cosmic Beings, would have that to be the case — that We would merely impart to you a Teaching and you would grasp it on the instant and respond from that moment forward with the full, innate understanding of that Teaching. But there is remaining within the momentums of most — not all — of mankind a great amount of density that does not allow for the first blush of our Instruction to be absorbed to the very core of their being.

Surely, your willingness to learn does prepare the vehicles of consciousness to be readied to receive that Initiation. It most certainly sets the focus of your consciousness to be keenly aware when that Initiation occurs. At such time, you are not startled or taken aback, but there is that sense of the ongoing striving toward the purpose of life which you have willingly entertained, and you embrace the Opportunity of the Initiation fully prepared to step through that cycle, so that you might understand even more fully every dimension that is to be imparted to you.

Initiation Affects All of Your Vehicles of Consciousness

Ofttimes, you will discover that each of the vehicles of consciousness is being trained through your Initiations. It is not merely a mental exercise of learning. The emotions will be tested. Is there sufficient Peace and disciplined Strength of the emotions? Is there sufficient energy within your vehicle to be able to stand fast during times of trial and stress? Do you have sufficient Illumination and Wisdom to see with the Christ Discriminating Faculties of the Mind of God those areas that would try to trick you or be stumbling blocks in your path to throw you off your point of centeredness so that you do not have the ability to hold fast to that Crucible of the Heart?

Would you find that you were in a state of reactionary motives rather than in the pensive, centered vibration of one who knows the right action and bides their time in the Poise of God Harmony? Or would you react precipitously, unprepared, allowing for the emotional body to send forth the slings and arrows of hatred or misqualified energy? Would you find that you would be able to hold your tongue and not speak, not lash out with harsh words, but stop and think first and place the Mind of your Holy Christ Presence into the equation? Having regained your Harmony, those harsh words would never be spoken. However, once spoken, they can never be taken back. You most assuredly can transmute that energy and you can call upon the Law of Forgiveness, but think of the grave hurt and scars that come forth by words unprotected by the Heart of a Christ.

When in doubt, you would be better to hold the tongue, never uttering a word, than to send forth any energy through the throat chakra that applies the energy of your own Crystal Cord into forming more karma that you are never sure will cease to have ramifications in your life or in the lives of others. This is why, beloved, it is so very important, as you enter into the Path of Initiation, to learn how to call forth the Light of your God Presence, to have that Light functioning through your energy centers so that you are fully vested with this Light of God, ready to move forward as the Christ.

Let Go of Attachment and Enter into the Heart of God

Many times on the Path of Initiation you will find another that you so desire to assist along the way. And try as you may, there is no response, for they have not heard the words nor felt the desire from within calling them Home. They have not understood the Wisdom calling them into the Home of the Heart. And though you have spent sufficient time moving through that cycle with this precious Flame of God whom you recognize, you cannot forever tarry, waiting for the Light to shine forth through them when there is no desire, no will to join you on the Path.

So a most difficult decision will arise. Can you be true to the Flame of God that is your True Identity, your Real Self, and stay in the proximity of one or more who would tear you from that Path? Or are you able to release the hold you have on the attachment to assisting another who will not respond, let go and place them in the Hands of their own God Presence, or in the Hands of the Ascended Ones, and be about the business of your Divine Self exercising the course of action required for your lifestream?

These Initiations are most difficult and ofttimes come when the initiate is closest to leaving behind the substance of their own human attachments and forging a closer communion with their own God Presence. Do not mistake my instructions regarding this Initiation. You are not called to leave hearth and home and family in order to come into the Heart of God. You are called to leave your attachments and come into the Heart of God. Do you see the difference, beloved? It is the attachments, the desiring of those things which you are not meant to control which is wrong. It is the mistaken, unfortunate effort to control those things which are not lawfully yours to command.

Placing your attention upon the Path of Initiation that is unfolding within your own lifestream is a great endeavor. This is why you are called upon to enter into the Heart, for within this Crucible of Being you can pass all Initiations presented to you. You can sort through all dilemmas, all concerns. You can find the Strength that is required to hold on when it would seem that you might not otherwise have all that is required, save that one *Thread of Contact* with the Heart of your God Presence. That is the *Thread,* come what may, to which you must hold fast, not letting go for an instant. For it will guide you through all Initiations, through all tests and struggles. For over that *Thread* passes the Current of your own God Presence — answering your calls, responding to your needs, filling your Heart, even should all about you disappear.

Maintaining Your Thread of Contact in this Era

To achieve their Victories in times past, it was required that initiates go off for long periods of time into the wilderness to learn what they were made of, to understand from whence come all things that they require in life. But this is not the pattern for the initiate in this era. For you can be actively living in a vast city with lifestreams all about you and still have the Initiation of the *Thread of Contact.* You need not climb the highest mountain of the Himalayas to find the rarefied atmosphere in which you may be closer to God. For the height of consciousness that you are required to traverse is right where you are this very moment.

We have prepared a place for you under the canopy of the Ascended and Cosmic Beings so that you might have a greater ease in elevating your consciousness and touching the Heart of the Ascended Ones. Oh, there are still those who would rather exercise their human ego and go off by themselves to some remote cavern and exercise their will to deprive the physical body, the emotional body, and the mental body, thinking that truly this is a godly path for one desiring the Agni of God.

Blessed hearts, move with the Consciousness present in the land that is light-years beyond those arcane methods of enlightenment. We have given much to assist you by way of Instruction, by Cups of Light of our own Consciousness, waiting for you to drink of the cup, digest it, assimilate it, and become it. As you are more able to let go of the attachments to those things spun out of your own human thought and feeling, the creations of the mayic illusion of the outer self, you will begin to sense, shining forth from your own Heart, the Wisdom of your own Christ Mind, the Love born of the Heart of your own God Presence, the Will aligned with that of your own I AM, and the ability to proclaim, "I AM" — for you will have embraced the Path of Initiation presented to you by your Holy Christ Presence.

The Initiation of the Cosmic Christ

Earlier, I spoke of the time when, having passed certain Initiations by unfurling the Threefold Flame of your Heart, there is sent forth to the Heart of your God Presence the resounding tone, "I AM Ready," and my Heart is receptive to that tone, receiving that signal. It is then time for my direct attention upon your Flame. As the Cosmic Christ, it is my honor to stand with you, to send forth the impetus of greater Teaching and Instruction that are revealed through the Threefold Flame of the Heart. Therefore, at the invitation of your own God Presence, I send forth certain directions, situations, and actions of the Heart that establish a Current whereby you are then drawn into the next level of Instruction according to that which you have already passed.

Know well, beloved, that if it feels as though you have been round and round with one or more Initiations many times, it is because you have not learned the intrinsic lesson required at the core of that Initiation. This is an example of why We, the Ascended and Cosmic Beings, send forth our Instruction through the Representatives — so that you might have that Teaching to illumine those areas of life that have not been clear before and for you to have a greater understanding of what you are to look for when the Initiation comes. I might add that, even should the lesson be the same, the Initiation will not always come forth in like manner as before. It may be masked as some other situation, and you may be caught off guard, thinking that surely you know how to traverse this circumstance, but you will have missed the very point of the Initiation and test.

Holding the Vision

This brings me to a most important point that I would like you to consider: You must hold the vision with vigilance and attention to detail so that you do not miss the very necessary aspect of life that has been specifically designed for you. Many Angels and Ascended Ones, not to say anything of your own God Presence and Holy Christ Presence, have gone to great lengths for you, the incarnate Son or Daughter of God, to have the Opportunity to enter into the stream of consciousness and flow of certain Initiations.

Do not mistake untransmuted returning karma for an Initiation because of your lack of attention to exercising the opportunity for transmutation, for they are not one and the same. But you might consider that were you to enter into the disciplines afforded you to invoke the Violet Flame, to invoke the Rays of God Consciousness and all of the God Qualities into your life, your opportunity would be eased considerably because returning karma would not then hinder your course and Initiation and you might move through them more easily.

Remember that I said the Initiations need not be difficult, but they require your attention. If you have your attention and all of the energy of your life available to this outer vehicle in a given day going hither and yon, spread too thin to be able to hold the balance for yourself, or you have a fleeting consciousness unable to maintain the center of attention to detail, you could suddenly realize you have forgotten the most important of details — the conscious awareness of the Crucible of Being. Then, beloved, the Initiations will be difficult.

So you see, even now, We lay out a course of study so that you might accelerate as quickly as the desire of your God Presence and the willingness of your heart will allow. As quickly as these outer vehicles willingly let go, you will discover the Christ descending into your life, accelerating your life, and marking each step with a Light that enables you to leave the Illumination of your own Initiation as the example that others might follow.

The Path of Initiation is a Blessing and a glorious Opportunity. You are on the Path, even when you do not choose to be, once you open your

Heart. So does it not make Christ Sense for you to accelerate on that Path willingly, cheerfully, filled with the Love and Gratitude for the Opportunity afforded your lifestream? Does this not afford you the Opportunity to enter into this Crucible of Being and allow that upraised Chalice to be filled to overflowing, so that you have more than enough for all of the mastery required of you and for the Heart to perform its Perfect Work extending God Service to others?

Blessed ones, when this occurs, you will know that God is ever so Perfect, for you will understand that there is no greater place to be than within the Heart — for there God abides, there God has always been, and there God will always be.

Embrace the Path of Initiation with an upraised Chalice and a joyful Heart, ready to see, to receive, and to experience the Fullness of your Christhood and of the I AM THAT I AM.

Be sealed in the Ruby Heart of my Flame, for I, Maitreya, hold you in my Heart. AUM. Perusha.

Lord Maitreya

When the Student is Ready, the Teacher Will Appear

Blessed Sons and Daughters of God, I, Maitreya, stand in your midst. Those of you aware of the Golden-Pink Waves of Light streaming forth from my Heart have already touched my Consciousness. You have received a Charge of Energy that streams forth from my Heart as I hold fast to the Truth of Cosmic Law®. I desire that Truth to go forth as Teaching and Instruction to bless the Sons and Daughters of God upon the Earth. I send forth my Ray of Consciousness in Waves of Light to capture the attention of those with an elevated Chalice ready to receive a higher understanding of a Higher Way of Life heretofore not in their conscious awareness.

Within every Son and Daughter of God there is the Seed of Purity and Fire that is immutable, that is Perfect. It holds the Individualized Identity of their God Presence. It is Consciousness in its purest form — the Consciousness of the Presence streaming forth as a pulse that will not be denied. But that which builds up around that Seed is ofttimes strewn with misperception, error in judgment, and misqualification. These intermingle with the streaming Consciousness that comes forth as the abounding Truth of the Law established for all by the Cosmic Consciousness of Ascended and Cosmic Beings who possess the Consciousness of the Mighty I AM.

Invoke the Light with Constancy for Yourself and Others

How then do you, as the sincere student, distinguish error, misqualification, even so-called evil, from Truth and from the Good that streams forth as Cosmic Law? The first step in the acceleration of your own consciousness, formed in and around the Truth of your Real Identity, begins when you can send forth a sufficient Spark of Light from the

Core of Being that attracts more of like nature unto itself and that rebukes and rebuffs those states of human consciousness unlike the true Core of Being.

Over many embodiments, you have delved into the curiosity of many human conditions spun out of misqualified thought and feeling. Perhaps in the beginning these miscreations were not your own but of another. And yet you nonetheless drank from the same cup and digested the same cesspool of negativity, thereby allowing it to give birth to error in judgment in your own consciousness.

Now the safeguard for the sincere student is in applying the law of striving and invoking the Light and the labor of Constancy for the common good. Allow for the Consciousness of those of Us who have won the Victory over time and space to saturate your consciousness, for We have taken God Command over human thought and feeling. We have built up bodies of Immortal Endurance. We have become the Purity of Cosmic Law through action, through deed, and through every thought streaming forth as our Ascended Consciousness.

You, blessed ones, are also building up such Immortal Vehicles of Light so that you might join the ranks of those Ascended — no more to have to struggle with these lesser vibrations of this dense world that catch you unaware when you let your guard down and do not sufficiently apply the pressure of the Flame that is the Purity of the Core of your Being into every endeavor.

When this Flame begins to ignite an awareness in a hungry soul yearning for the Light, yearning for the Truth of the Law, hungry for the Teaching, then, blessed ones, the Teacher will appear. In the beginning it may be a friend, a co-worker, a relative; it may be a stranger you pass on the street who imparts Words of Wisdom that strike a chord, reminding you of that Flame and of your pursuit, satisfying your hunger for a moment. But once that moment has passed and that cycle fulfilled, the hunger returns, the thirst remains, and it is as though you were walking through the parched desert with nothing in sight to satisfy your yearning.

So you continue to strive and return once more to the Heart, allowing for the Flame upon the Altar to have your attention, to be nourished by that attention. For that attention focuses the flow of energy, streaming forth daily from your God Presence back into your consciousness, there to be qualified by the upraised Chalice of the White Fire Core of your Being as the Truth of your God Self. Then there is opportunity to build upon that which you have just learned, that which has been a remembrance of perhaps a time long past, which encourages you to strive on and continue your search.

Then, as more Light is generated as Consciousness, as Purity, you push forward into the ability to be open should the Teacher appear. And that openness, blessed ones, is a great Victory indeed. For absent your ability to allow the Flame of your own True Identity to expand sufficiently for you to be open and receptive to the Teacher, there is no room for the Teacher. The Teacher will not appear until you are ready.

The Appearance of the Teacher

This brings us to the appearance of the Teacher. How do you receive the Teacher? Is it with doubt, with mistrust? Is there an area in your consciousness that so relates to the untransmuted misperceptions of life or the errors in judgment of your past actions, thoughts, and feelings that you sit in judgment and question whether or not the Teacher truly has the Mantle required for your acceleration up the Ladder of Life? In that critical attitude, once more the Teacher must step aside and allow your own returning karma, the trial and error buffeting of time and space to be your teacher.

You can say that your attention has long been upon these Teachings and that you have striven to be a very good person, not harming any part of life. But has your effort accelerated your consciousness to your full potential here and now? Are you fully engaged in the Stream of Consciousness as Waves of the Golden-Pink Light of Illumination's Flame stream forth from the Heart of a World Teacher? Can I even now enfold you and accelerate you into a new Consciousness, into a new way to formulate thought founded upon the firm foundation of the

Identity of your True State of Being, the Mighty I AM?

The key to entering into such communion with the Teacher is trust. Absent that trust, the door is not open. There is not the opportunity for the Light to stream forth, saturating your consciousness so that the Truth of your Being might be accelerated into Higher Attainment, building a momentum that allows for the Victory, assuring your Ascension.

That trust which I have touched upon is the very foundation of Hierarchy, which to some is a fearful word indeed. For they fear putting into the Flame the misconceptions of their life, the misqualification of the energy sown into their own consciousness, and the lie that has been consciously appropriated as their own. For trust in Hierarchy to appear, all of that must go into the Flame.

So many students fail to move beyond a certain plateau of the ladder. They are literally incapable of climbing into that Higher Vibration required for the full expression of Christhood due to self-imposed limitations. So they stay upon that plateau, not advancing, not accelerating, but finding themselves ever more drawn back into the human creation of their own consciousness and, ultimately, far removed from where they began. Doubt in the Teacher erodes the very consciousness that would otherwise accelerate them into the Higher Vehicles of their own True Identity, building a momentum that would have assured their Victory.

Now you begin to understand how the trickery of your own human ego can erode the very Christhood you would otherwise have adopted so readily were not seeds of mistrust and doubt allowed to foster even greater errors in your own judgment and discerning faculties. Many voices in the land desire to attract you and espouse their byways. At best, most of these paths deal with the expansion of temporal areas that cannot lead to the acceleration of your own Christ Attainment. It is one thing to expand your consciousness in pursuit of your Destiny. But relying on your outer intellect to reach your Destiny is not what is required by your Mighty I AM Presence for genuine Attainment. If lessons are to be learned pursuing certain areas of worldly responsibility, surely this experience will give you co-measurement between yourself and those worldly professionals swimming in an astral sea of duality, separated from their Mighty I AM Presence and attunement in the Christ.

There are others who follow the Star of their True Identity of the Mighty I AM Presence, who listen to Hierarchy, who receive the Consciousness charged with the Light of the Ascended Realms, and who allow this absorption into their world through an open Heart so their own Holy Christ Presence may step forth. And in those areas of life where Initiation ensues, Hierarchy — the Consciousness of the Ascended and Cosmic Beings and of your own Mighty I AM Presence — is there to keep the watch so that you will not wander far astray and engage untransmuted substance that still remains in your own consciousness. Then the energy you continue to accumulate in your life accelerates in Purity, in the fulfillment of that which strives toward the common good, and, most especially, in building the Chalice where your own God Presence may send forth the Mind of

God to impress upon life those Ideals born only in the Heart of God and that will establish an acceleration of consciousness, not merely for your own lifestream, but for all the Sons and Daughters of God upon the Earth.

The Lessons of History

If you consider the last two thousand years and the scientific advances of mankind, has there really been an acceleration of consciousness, or has it been an intellectual Tower of Babel? Are more Chalices prepared for the Ascension? Are the masses of humanity continuing to accelerate? Or has there been a degeneration of consciousness among mankind?

These are serious considerations for the Sons and Daughters of God. For every thought that goes forth is establishing consciousness, is building upon energy that is already accumulated. Is that which you are building, blessed ones, founded upon the Temple of the Most High? Or is there still remaining the soiled consciousness that seizes upon the precious Purity of your Electrons of

Light, misqualifies them, and adds to the sum total of human thought and feeling building upon the Earth? We have given many Instructions on how to clear these planes of consciousness of the pollution of misqualified energy. You know how to make the call. You know how to invoke the Holy Angels to expand your calls. But do you know how to arrest further pollution of human thought and feeling in your own world instead of adding to the collective negativity?

It is not enough to be calling for the Light on one hand and on the other to undermine that conscious command with the doubts, fears, and human questioning of the ego. This will ultimately erode the budding Christ Consciousness of the most sincere student on the Path. Guard well against that serpentine murmuring which you entertain, for not only will you be required to balance that karma, blessed ones, but you will be feeding into the collective karma of a planet already in need of salvation.

The development of worldly achievements over the last few hundred years should show you how mankind can and do take the Light of God and fashion it into all manner of pursuits for good or ill. They are the fruit of an impersonal Law of Creation that cannot be denied to anyone who has the ability to cognize thought. So, too, the very acceleration of the planet can be achieved by the Sons and Daughters of God who will put their attention upon the Most High, who will stay receptive to the Teacher and the Teaching, who will hear the Voice and Vibration of the Ascended and Cosmic Beings, who radiate Light into their world, quickening the very foundation of the Earth.

Remaining Tethered to Hierarchy Assures Victory

Sons and Daughters of God, if you desire to enter into World Service and begin to penetrate through the density built up over the Seed of Purity within you, then you must become a whirling Star of accelerating vibration into your own Mighty I AM Presence. You must allow your open Heart to continue to tether you to the "Ladder of Life" known as Hierarchy so that you can have the reinforcement, the multiplication, and the

Instruction in a timely manner when We deem it necessary, not only for your own lifestream and attainment, but for the common good.

This, blessed ones, is how you bring about a Golden Age. My Words may be cast aside and lost to the outer ear in generations to come, but the Instruction will remain. The Vibration of Consciousness that streams forth from the Hearts of the Ascended and Cosmic Beings sets forth the Truth of the Law. The permanent Akashic Records of these Dictations shall continue to sound the Cosmic Tone that can only issue forth from the foundation of God Reality.

Should you find that you continue to insist on trusting the Teacher on one hand and entering into doubt on the other hand, then examine more closely the Teaching that has challenged your substance. Search what it is that has incited your doubt in that Instruction. If you can be severely honest with yourself, you will discover the key that will accelerate your consciousness into the Truth of the Law, revealing the Thread of Truth that has always been and will always remain. The Teaching will not overturn that which has stood the test of time, which has stood as Cosmic Law established by Alpha and Omega — not as established by the human intellect and feeling evolving upon a planet still immersed in negativity. You will find that when you discover these Threads of Truth, you will be required to look within your own consciousness to find that which has sown the seeds of doubt and worse — betrayal — betrayal that has taken you far afield from where you desire to be.

Blessed ones, the hunger and thirst that began the sojourn into the acceleration for your Ascension is a beginning step. Then the real work begins. For you cannot think that once you find the Teacher, that once the Teaching has begun to dawn upon your own consciousness and be internalized, that suddenly you have won the day — perhaps the moment, but not the day and not the race. For determination and the striving of the Heart are required for you to stay the course until the completion of your Victory. There are layers and layers of human consciousness that must be transmuted before the Pure Flame of your Identity can be revealed to not only your own consciousness, but, yes, to the rest of the world. Only then can those about you recognize the Fullness of the Pure Light of God shining forth. Only then will it be evident that you truly bend the knee before that Light, that you no longer carry that self-concern or egotism of one who yet remains burdened with untransmuted human creation at the fore of their consciousness.

Yes, it is a process, and, yes, it takes time, and, yes, you must have Patience, not only with your fellow sojourners but with yourself, so that you will stay the course, so that you will sustain the precious *Thread of Contact* that allows for the reinforcement to keep you inviolate, strong, so that you might have the Courage to move forward. And so as that consciousness not aligned with the Truth of your Being is revealed to you, you can fearlessly consign that consciousness into the Flame. Allow it to be transmuted and erased from the record of time so that only Purity qualifies the Energy flowing from your God Presence, building upon the foundation of your True Identity. This is how great Causal Body Momentums are built in every life.

Heretofore there has not been such open Instruction to the masses whose consciousness would arouse virulent opposition of human thought and feeling as the enemy of Truth. Thus, the Mystery Schools have been reserved for sincere students who have already won a tremendous Victory over themselves. If the Sons and Daughters of God do not guard well this assistance of Hierarchy, there may come a time when it is necessary to draw a cloak of invisibility over our Fires released for the sincere students of the Light.

Then the Earth would once more move into a dark age where there is not the free exchange of the High Ideals and the visible Waves of Light streaming forth from Hierarchy to accelerate all who are upon the planet. Throughout past ages, cycles have come and cycles have gone. You know this from recorded history. Each time we have initiated World Religions, there have always been those naysayers who arise to distract or misdirect the attention of those ready to receive the new World Religion.

Enter into the Figure-Eight Flow with the Teacher Now!

Blessed hearts, I, Maitreya, know well the consciousness that is within your Heart. I likewise know well the tendencies of your own karmic patterns that would pull you in various directions away from the Polestar of your True Being. This can occur if there is not the acceleration of your consciousness and vibration to a high enough pitch to sufficiently throw off the world's human thought and feeling and to keep your attention fixed upon your Mighty I AM. Through this acceleration, the Tone that streams forth from your own Heart Flame will not only reach out from your own spherical awareness, but it will reverberate throughout the land because you have an emotional body that is under God Control and charged sufficiently with Light. This acceleration comes about, blessed ones, not only because you have entered into the figure-eight flow with the Light and Consciousness of the Ascended Masters, making yourself available for that which is the common good, but because you have also elected to put your own human thought and feeling and your own human ego into the Violet Flame and to continually call that Flame forth so there is no self save your God Self within you.

Perhaps you think I exaggerate and that my words merely paint with a broad brush a landscape for tomorrow or the day after and that surely it is not this day and this company of which I speak. But it would be folly to entertain anything less than a solemn response to my admonition and to accepting this Release and Teaching.

You, blessed ones, must begin to exercise the Responsibility for that which you must fulfill. Though you need Hierarchy and Hierarchy will need to be a part of your ongoing life until your Ascension, you are simultaneously becoming independent in your own Christhood. And this is the problem for most of the Sons and Daughters of God, for they do not understand how to develop the Fullness of their Christ Discrimination and become the Individualization of the Mighty I AM Presence and still hold fast to the Teacher. It is simple, blessed ones. The Teacher never acts contrary to that which is in congruence with your own Mighty I AM Presence, which is always the highest good for your lifestream.

For you to have the full weight of Authority over your own lifestream, you must first gain sufficient tethering to your own God Presence. For this to be accomplished, you must enter into the figure-eight flow with the Teacher, establishing trust in the Teaching and the Message that comes forth from the Anointed Representatives. Then, blessed ones, you begin to establish the multiplication factor that is required for the streaming Consciousness that you have been caught up in this day to continue to accelerate your own consciousness.

I repeat, many of you are aware of the streaming Light of Consciousness pulsating forth from this Release. For those not able to enter into the subtle nature of this Consciousness or to be sufficiently aware of that pulsation, I say to you: Strive and continue to strive with every erg of energy of your being; bend the knee before your own God Presence in supplication to allow the Teacher to return into your life once more; allow your Heart to be open to the Representatives so that there will be a sufficient Touchstone of Reality to keep you tethered; allow for the Light of God to sweep through your consciousness as Violet Transmuting Flame to consume your every doubt, your every fear, and all human questioning, betrayal, rebellion, resistance — and yes, even treachery — that might be ingrained within your garments.

Know well, blessed ones, that betrayal and treachery are the worst offenses to life. Do not find yourself caught in such a spiral, for you will assure yourself of several more rounds of embodiments. Allow for the Fullness of the Truth of the Seed of your Pure Identity as the Mighty I AM Presence upon the Altar of your Heart to take dominion over your life, to consciously qualify the Energy of God that builds upon your foundation, and to have that foundation firmly fixed as the Temple of the Most High Living God. Then you will find that any opposing force seeking to establish itself as a cornerstone in your foundation will not be able to take hold, for your foundation will not allow any negativity to express itself. As quickly as there is a flash of thought or energy moving in your vehicles of consciousness contrary to the Highest Ideals of the Teaching and Vibration of the Teacher, call upon the Light of Saint Germain, of El Morya, of the Goddess of Light, and, yes, of my Flame. I promise that your calls will be answered. And if you are willing to let go of that human condition, it will be gone in a flash, for your call will compel the answer. But you must consciously and sincerely desire to be rid of that human substance once and for all.

What Do You Believe at the Core of Your Being?

The Light of God can never fail. But do you believe it? Have you adopted this as an article of Faith? Have you established sufficient trust in the Teaching and the Teacher to know that the Light of God is truly the Allness of Being and that your Individualized Mighty I AM Presence stands as the Authority over these outer vehicles that you wear? Have you truly understood to the core of your being that what you think, what you feel, and the actions which you undertake do affect all of life and that you are responsible for that energy?

Do you believe you can transmute any sense of limitation with that Never-Failing Light of God? Do you believe that all that you require, all that you must learn, all that you must become comes forth from your own God Presence?

These are fundamental questions that you should ask yourself over and over again. For from time to time, you will be called upon to testify to your own God Presence and to surrender your entire being into the Flame of God. It is that surrender that allows for the acceleration of your attainment and mastery. Without that total surrender there is not acceleration, and the Mighty I AM Presence is obliged to suffer you to continue to move through the consciousness of your intellect and emotions absent the Illumination of the Mind of God.

Respond on the Instant to the Command of the Teacher

This is why you need the Teacher, for the Teacher reminds you. If you are to stand in the Fullness of the integration with your God Presence and the Teacher desires to teach you how to respond on the instant to the Command of the Presence, does it not stand to reason that you should respond on the instant to the Command of the Teacher? And is it not the Responsibility of the Teacher to exact that discipline and require it of the disciple?

This is an important lesson to master. For it is part of the training that will enable you to be in the right place at the right time — not only for the fulfillment of your Divine Plan, but for your integration with Hierarchy, for a greater acceleration of consciousness into all that is Pure, all that is Holy, that knows itself to be the Mighty I AM Presence, and that can be a part of the Allness of God. But when consciousness is not responsive to the Command, then, blessed ones, rebellion is at the core. Negative thought and feeling, misperception of life, and rampant misqualification disfigure your consciousness.

Know then that when the Light of your Mighty I AM Presence is firmly fixed in your world you do not lose one erg of energy or one firm footprint in the sands of time, and you are able to respond immediately to the Command of the Teacher. The reason for this is that you are upheld in the Fullness of the Stream of Light that is the Allness of Being. You are held and nurtured in that embrace. Your consciousness as thought and feeling and the physical body you wear are ultimately content in that Divine Embrace. When sufficient transmutation has occurred, there is no longer the squabbling of human thought and feeling resisting the embrace of the Allness of God.

That which I have taught this day may for some require the work of an entire embodiment or more to accept and to master. Others are required to embrace and establish this Instruction quickly if they are not to lose the momentum and opportunity to fulfill their Divine Plan in this very embodiment. The record shows that there are always those who rebel against the Teaching and decide they know better than the Teacher, than the Representatives. Even when we have stood directly before these individuals, giving them the Fullness of our Light, our Consciousness, and our Instruction, they have turned away.

Yes, blessed hearts, there are many paths, and many do indeed gravitate to their own levels of comfortability in deciding what they are willing to accept in their consciousness or as their touchstone of "reality." True, those lifestreams will find their way eventually — but is that excuse enough for turning away from the Ascended Masters, for not embracing their Anointed Representatives, or for not establishing the trust attested by Hearts embraced in the Conscious Wave of Ascended Master Light streaming forth as in this very moment? And yet, when individuals are removed from our close embrace, will they be content to gravitate back to their own human thought and feeling?

Your Response Determines the Closeness of the Ascended Masters

You, blessed ones, are the test case of whether or not the Ascended Masters can continue to come this close, of whether or not the consciousness of sufficient numbers of Sons and Daughters of God is ready to receive this Fire, of whether or not there will be a return to the enveloping darkness of ages past when the Halls of Learning and Higher Consciousness will be closed to all save the accomplished few.

You are the test. Mark well that wherever you are, whether here in this Sanctuary or elsewhere across the Earth this day, you know to whom I speak. You know that the test is now and the Initiation from Maitreya is upon you.

As you receive this Light, know that the impersonal action of the Blessing on all who are Pure in Heart goes forth until they are able consciously to receive a greater understanding of this Instruction. Know that I, Maitreya, will continue to stand with the Sons and Daughters of God upon the Earth for hundreds of years to come, if necessary, devising new ways in which the Consciousness of God may stream forth sufficiently to accelerate these Sons and Daughters into their own Ascension in the Light. The Initiations and cycles of each generation take on a slightly different complexion, but know well that the Vibration of the Thread of Truth forever remains the same.

I trust the Flame that is ablaze upon the Altar of your Heart and in the pressure of the Consciousness of your own God Presence desiring your Victory. I trust that the Teaching we are delivering through these Representatives will be internalized sufficiently to accelerate your consciousness into the Fullness of your own God Presence and that your Victory of the Ascension will come forth.

I trust in the Fullness of the Christ that has the Mind of God streaming forth, depositing that Consciousness sufficiently to begin to establish that Reality within your own vehicles of expression.

Let that Consciousness soar. Let the open Heart continue to receive the Teaching and the Teacher. And let the Light of God be God Victorious over all of the affairs of your life.

Maitreya

Carolyn L. Shearer, Anointed Representative®
Closing Comments on the Dictation:

When the Student is Ready, the Teacher Will Appear

Maitreya has said that there are a few lifestreams who will have difficulty with his Release. I invite you to write to us if there is a concern on your Heart as to how to begin to understand what he has said, or if there are questions about Cosmic Law that we might address, either by responding directly or by pointing you in the direction of previous Releases on certain topics that you are still wrestling with.

The Masters have long said they do not want reluctant chelas, for they can accomplish more with a few who, in a concerted momentum, focus the Consciousness of the Mighty I AM, than with stragglers who don't know whether or not they desire to get into the Clipper Ship with Maitreya.

This is an opportunity for those of you who still have difficult issues within your consciousness to have those issues addressed. Should there be similar questions posed by many of you, questions on the same or related points of the Law, those questions will be addressed publicly. For if there are more than a few who do not understand a particular Teaching, then we need to teach it again. I do hope that you understand that Monroe and I, as the Anointed Representatives of the Brotherhood, stand ready to serve your spiritual needs. That is our Holy Purpose.

If you continue to stuff those needs and do not bring them to the light of day, allowing those pent-up misunderstandings or confusions about the Teachings to be harbored — you heard what Maitreya said: It will eventually erode that which would otherwise be a firm foundation to accelerate you on your Path in this lifetime.

There are a few momentous Releases that the Masters have dictated through us to the students over the tenure of our Messengership.

All are important. But this Release is of highest importance to new and old students alike, for it is the nexus point of your ability to accomplish more of what your God Presence desires you to accomplish.

Monroe and I both hope you will avail yourself of this opportunity to obtain clarification regarding anything that is a stumbling block on your Path. Short of sitting down hour by hour with each one of you across the planet, this is the time, and this is the hour. I hope that you will continue to apply the disciplines and the practices of the Teachings you are learning so that when questions come up, you work with them for a while, discover the answer from your study of the Teachings, and then move on with your gaze and your vision to the future.

Far too many are concerned with living in the past. Although we study history and Teachings that have come down through antiquity, which hold to this high Vibration of the Masters' Teachings, you are not required to go back and continue to feed into the old momentums, the old habits, and the old records of your own human creation or that of others. For if you are looking back, surely you are not looking forward. And if you are not looking forward, there is not the accelerated gaze upon the goal, which is the Ascension.

We have many recordings. Everything that has been released through us by the Masters has been recorded to date. They are not one time Releases. They are for your study. They are for you to pore over and continue to rehearse in your own consciousness, to learn the Teaching and become that Teaching. I do hope you will avail yourselves of as many recordings and as much time for study of these Releases as possible, for you will find that your own attunement with your Mighty I AM Presence will guide you to the particular Releases you need at particular times.

We are working toward getting more of that Instruction and Teaching transferred into print, for we do understand the necessity to be able to read it and study it line by line. We have a limited staff, there are only twenty-four hours in a day, and we do have many demands on our little band of mighty lifestreams who are here. But in time, more Releases will be converted into print for those of you who find that an easier way to study. But that should not keep you from rehearing the Releases.

When those Releases are replayed, you need to know that the Light originally released by the Masters comes with it. And, yes, the I AM Presence of the Representatives is also engaged in that Release every time it is replayed. Monroe and I know in a very precise and yet subtle way when there are students pulling on particular Releases. If we happen to be away from the platform for a Sunday Service and there is a replay of a Release, we are in the Fire of that Rerelease.

Take advantage of the opportunity! Take advantage of the opportunity! I can't say that enough. The Masters have said it. Now we as the Representatives say it. Take advantage of the opportunity!

You have to know that we love you. There are easier ways to go through life and win your Ascension than being an Anointed Representative, but neither one of us would trade our role on this stage of life for any of our other lifetimes. For it only takes one overshadowing Presence of the Masters to make it all worthwhile. It only takes one of you making your Ascension to make it all worthwhile. We work together, you and we, along with the Ascended Masters, and we are all climbing up this ladder. It used to be known as Jacob's Ladder. Well, Jacob is still right here beside me climbing the ladder with us.

Don't become lazy in your sojourn. It does require a lot of energy. It requires work. But nothing you have ever accomplished that has been good and rewarding in your life has been accomplished without effort. That striving is the motor of accelerating attainment. If you ever doubted that, just pick up any one of the Agni Yoga books, and you'll read it on every other page — labor, labor, labor. It does not mean that you are subservient to those in the world in your labor, but that you are laboring in striving for the common good of the Allness of God.

Thank you for your kind attention.

We welcome you to become a
Torch Bearer of The Temple®
in a Sacred Covenant with
Beloved Saint Germain and
the Brotherhood's Mission through
The Temple of The Presence.®

If you would like more information on
becoming a Torch Bearer or on
The Temple of The Presence,
please call us at
520-751-2039
or visit our website at
www.templeofthepresence.org.

You are also invited to connect with us
on Facebook and Instagram.

We are so grateful you have heard the Words of the Ascended Masters and have recognized the Light of their Consciousness going forth into the world.

TORCH BEARERS®
THE TEMPLE OF THE PRESENCE